UNDERSTANDING PROMPT ENGINEERING

DR DHEERAJ MEHROTRA

Made with ♥ on the Notion Press Platform
www.notionpress.com

Contents

Preface

In recent years, natural language processing (NLP) has witnessed tremendous growth, and with it, the task of language understanding has gained considerable attention. Among the crucial components of NLP systems, prompt engineering is one of the most significant. Prompts are the text inputs the language model receives, guiding it to generate the desired output.

Creating effective prompts is critical in developing any NLP system for conversational AI, question answering, or text classification. Despite its significance, prompt engineering is a less explored area in NLP, and there is a lack of comprehensive resources that focus on this topic.

This book aims to bridge this gap by providing a comprehensive overview of prompt engineering. It covers the fundamental concepts of prompt engineering and offers practical guidelines and examples for creating effective prompts. The book also discusses different approaches to prompt engineerings, such as template-based, natural language, and mixed-initiative prompts.

In addition, this book provides an in-depth analysis of various evaluation metrics used to assess the effectiveness of prompts. It also covers the latest research trends and future directions in prompt engineering.

This book is intended for researchers, practitioners, and students interested in NLP and prompt engineering. It assumes some familiarity with NLP and machine learning concepts but is accessible to readers from diverse backgrounds. We hope this book will serve as a valuable resource and contribute to advancing the field of prompt engineering.

Author

www.authordheerajmehrotra.com

ONE

Prompt Engineering- The New Age Skill

Prompt Engineering is a talent becoming vital in today's fast-paced and ever-changing employment environment. Prompt Engineering is a skill that is becoming increasingly necessary. This competency emphasizes the capacity to solve issues rapidly and effectively and make judgments promptly. Prompt engineering is becoming an increasingly helpful tool for those interested in increasing their employability and achieving tremendous professional success in their chosen fields as new technologies and breakthroughs emerge.

To get to the heart of prompt engineering, one must be able to react to problems and difficulties as they arise in real-time. This may include various activities, from resolving a technical issue on the spot to making meaningful choices with less notice. To succeed in this industry, one has to have several abilities and attributes that allow one to move swiftly and decisively in various situations.

The capacity to think critically and analytically is one of the most essential talents necessary for prompt engineering. This requires having the ability to make a prompt and correct assessment of a situation, followed by the formulation of a solution that targets the underlying source of the issue. Since it enables people to detect possible hurdles and devise methods for overcoming them, critical thinking is a crucial component of prompt engineering. This is because critical thinking is an essential component of prompt engineering.

Communication is another crucial talent that is necessary for rapid engineering. This requires not just the capacity to explain thoughts and solutions clearly and succinctly but also the capacity to listen actively and with empathy to others. Good communication is essential in any setting involving the working of a team. Still, it is of utmost significance in rapid engineering because it enables employees to work together effectively and cooperatively.

The rapid engineering methodology strongly emphasises adaptation and flexibility, which is one of the most beneficial characteristics of the method. It is necessary for those working in this industry to have the ability to swiftly adapt to new conditions and methods due to the rapid pace at which both business practices and technological advancements are advancing. This may require anything from acquiring new technical skills to reevaluating objectives in response to changing circumstances in the market.

A few fundamental abilities are helpful in the new age and mainly apply to rapid engineering. These are the following:

The ability to analyze and comprehend giant data sets has become an increasingly crucial talent in various sectors due to the emergence of big data and analytics. Those with prior expertise in data analysis are often in high demand in multiple industries, including banking, healthcare, and marketing.

Cybersecurity: The risks to the integrity of data and networks continue to increase in tandem with the progression of technology. Cybersecurity experts are in great demand across practically all business sectors as companies work to secure their data and assets from the hands of criminals.

Agile development uses agile approaches, gaining popularity in software development and project management. These strategies emphasize adaptability, teamwork, and continual improvement; hence, they work well in contexts that need quick engineering.

Cloud computing has become an integral component of many enterprises because it enables them to store data and apps remotely and access them anywhere. Experienced cloud computing professionals are in great demand as many businesses transfer their activities online. "the cloud" is becoming the preferred location for business operations.

The term "design thinking" refers to a method of problem-solving that emphasizes empathy, cooperation, and creative thinking. Since it inspires people to think creatively and develop original answers to complex problems, it is especially well-suited to workplaces that need quick engineering. This is because it pushes individuals to think creatively and beyond the box.

In addition to these particular abilities, several more general talents and characteristics are essential for those who want to succeed in prompt engineering. These are the following:

Resilience: Rapid engineering situations may be fast-paced and high-pressure, and employees must retain a good attitude and remain focused even when adverse conditions occur.

Curiosity: Those willing to learn and always want to expand their knowledge tend to be the most effective prompt engineers. They constantly seek new knowledge and ways of doing things and do not fear experimenting with or trying new things.

The ability to think quickly and creatively on one's feet is essential for prompt engineers since they must be able to solve unforeseen problems with original ideas. They can overcome challenges and accomplish their objectives using the resources and knowledge they already possess.

Collaboration: Working together on a project is one of the most important aspects of being on a team.

Hence, Skilling through prompt engineering means using specific instructions (called "prompts") to train an AI model to perform a specific task or improve its performance on a particular type of input. These prompts guide the model's behaviour and help it learn more effectively. By using prompts, we can train AI models to perform tasks better and more efficiently than traditional methods.

TWO

Approaches to Prompt Engineering

A methodology known as "Prompt Engineering" emphasizes the capability of swiftly and effectively finding solutions to challenges and making timely choices. Prompt engineering is becoming an important tool for AI users who wish to improve their decision-making processes due to the growing use of artificial intelligence (AI) in various sectors. This trend may be attributed to the proliferation of AI usage across numerous industries. Users of AI have access to several different prompt engineering strategies that may assist them in efficiently solving challenges.

Data analysis is one of the most significant aspects of prompt engineering, and it is also one of the most essential methodologies. It is crucial to have data that is both accurate and relevant to be able to make choices quickly and intelligently. Users of AI have access to various tools, including data visualization, statistical analysis, and machine learning algorithms, which may help them evaluate vast volumes of data in a timely and effective manner. They can recognize patterns, trends, and anomalies that may not be obvious at first glance by carrying out these steps. This knowledge may be used to improve the quality of decision-making processes and the efficiency with which issues are solved.

The second essential step in accelerating the engineering process is to generate a list of priorities. When confronted with several difficulties or obstacles, it may be difficult to decide where one's attention should be focused. AI users can make more educated judgments and more efficient use of their resources if they determine their priorities based on criteria such as the degree of urgency, significance, and possible influence of a given situation. Prioritization may also assist in discovering problems that can be handled quickly and simply, enabling AI users to concentrate their attention on issues that are more difficult or time-consuming to tackle.

Specifying objectives: Specifying precise objectives is another essential step in fast engineering. AI users may develop a clear path for their decision-making processes if they set SMART objectives. SMART goals are precise, measurable, attainable, relevant and time-bound goals. This might help them concentrate their time and resources on finding solutions to challenges that are in line with the broader goals they have set for themselves. Establishing objectives may also assist in identifying probable hurdles and problems, enabling AI users to prepare for contingencies and make better-informed choices. Defining goals can also aid users of AI.

Taking a proactive approach Using an aggressive strategy is another essential component of prompt engineering. Prompt engineering is characterized by its speed and efficiency. AI users may adopt a proactive approach by recognizing possible difficulties and fixing them before they become serious problems rather than waiting for problems to occur and then addressing them when they do occur. This may entail implementing preventative measures such as system backups, redundant systems, and planning for disaster recovery. A second aspect of being proactive is recognizing areas where there is room for development and then actively working to enhance operational procedures and infrastructure to forestall the occurrence of issues in the first place.

Working in tandem with other people is yet another essential component of practical quick engineering. Solving complicated issues often calls for contributions from various stakeholders, each of whom brings unique skills to the table. Users of AI can more effectively harness their pooled knowledge and abilities to find solutions to challenges if they work together with other users. Collaborating may also assist in recognizing any blind spots and ensure that all relevant considerations are considered when making judgments.

As a user of AI, prompt engineering may assist you in solving challenges more efficiently in several different ways. To begin, data analysis enables you to locate patterns and trends expediently and effectively, which may help guide your decision-making processes. This may help you spot possible difficulties before they become serious problems. It can also assist you in making better-educated choices based on accurate and pertinent data.

Second, you can direct most of your energy and resources toward resolving the most critical problems if you list priorities and clearly define your objectives. You will be able to make progress on the issues that are most essential to your business if you do not let yourself get distracted or weighed down by less significant difficulties as a result of doing this.

Finally, if you take a proactive approach, you may stop issues from occurring in the first place by preventing them from developing. This may entail implementing preventative measures such as system backups, redundancy, and disaster recovery plans, identifying potential for improvement and optimising both processes and systems.

Last but not least, if you work with other people to tackle complex challenges, you may use your team's pooled expertise and experience to do so more successfully. With collaboration, possible blind spots may be uncovered, and one can better guarantee that all relevant considerations are considered when making judgments.

THREE

Prompt Effectiveness

In the context of prompt engineering, the capacity to swiftly and effectively find solutions to issues and make choices in a timely way is referred to as prompt effectiveness. This is a phrase that is used in the context of prompt engineering. To do this, it is necessary to use several strategies, such as data analysis, establishing priorities and goals, proactive planning, and cooperative effort. The realm of artificial intelligence places a premium on prompt effectiveness because it allows users of AI technology to make educated choices that are founded on data that is both accurate and relevant, as well as to solve issues in a way that is both more expedient and effective.

For AI, rapid and effective response is vital for several reasons. First, artificial intelligence systems produce massive volumes of data, which need immediate analysis and decision-making. Users of artificial intelligence can go through this data and discover patterns and trends that may not be obvious at first glance because to prompt engineering. This may assist businesses in making informed judgments and help them improve their AI systems so that they function at their best.

Second, if there is a problem or outage with the system, fast engineering is necessary. If an AI system malfunctions, immediate efficacy is essential for reducing the blackout's impact and resuming regular operations as fast as feasible. AI users can spot possible difficulties and take action to avoid them from becoming big problems if they adopt a proactive approach, define priorities, and construct a hierarchy of concerns.

Finally, efficiency promptly is essential in the context of developing technologies such as self-driving cars and smart cities. These technologies produce enormous volumes of data, which need a speedy analysis and determination-making process. It is possible, with the aid of prompt engineering, to guarantee that these technologies run safely and efficiently and that any issues are swiftly discovered and rectified.

In the area of cybersecurity, quick efficacy is a crucial component. AI systems must be able to react rapidly and effectively to possible dangers since cyber attacks are becoming more complex. The use of prompt engineering may assist in the identification of potential vulnerabilities and the implementation of measures to avoid the occurrence of cyber assaults.

In conclusion, prompt effectiveness is a crucial component of prompt engineering, and it is necessary for AI users who want to maximize the effectiveness of their decision-making processes and find solutions to challenges in a more timely and productive manner. AI users may obtain optimum outcomes and guarantee that their AI systems run securely and effectively by using a variety of strategies such as data analysis, priority setting, goal definition, proactivity, and cooperation. These strategies can be used to AI.

FOUR

Significance of Prompt Engineering

The ever-increasing dependence on technology and data is one of the primary factors contributing to the growing importance of Prompt Engineering in the modern world. Discovering, assessing, and finding timely and efficient solutions is called "Prompt Engineering." It is necessary to handle and analyze this data in a timely way and efficiently to extract insights and make choices influenced by this data to keep up with the fast-rising quantity of data created every day. The following is a list of some of the most important reasons why Prompt Engineering is essential in the modern world:

Quick Engineering assists businesses in being more effective in their operations by rapidly locating and fixing any issues that may arise. Consequently, this leads to a reduction in downtime, an increase in production, and an improvement in customers' happiness.

Data analysis: Since a massive quantity of data is produced daily, it is very necessary to process and analyze this data promptly to extract insights and make choices based on accurate information. With the help of Prompt Engineering, businesses can process and analyze data in record time, therefore gaining valuable insights that can be used to improve their operations.

Economic savings may be realized when businesses can decrease the need for costly repairs and costly downtime by swiftly detecting and resolving issues as they arise. Over time, this may result in considerable cost reductions.

Prompt Engineering assists companies in making better choices by providing them with timely and correct data, which in turn enables the company to make better decisions. Because of this, they may be able to increase their overall performance and the efficiency of their operations.

Risk management: In light of the ever-increasing complexity of modern technology and the ever-present danger posed by cyberattacks, it is necessary to recognize and respond to any possible risks swiftly. Prompt Engineering can assist businesses in identifying potential threats and developing responses to address those threats before they escalate into serious issues.

Innovation: Prompt Engineering may also help enterprises innovate by rapidly finding new possibilities and producing new goods or services tailored to their clientele's requirements. This helps businesses better serve their clients.

In a nutshell, the ever-increasing need for technology and data drives the growing importance of prompt engineering in the modern world. Prompt Engineering may assist businesses in remaining competitive and achieving their objectives by facilitating the rapid identification and resolution of issues, processing and examining data, forming improved judgments, and introducing innovative ideas.

FIVE

Prompt Engineering & Employable Youth

Prompt engineering, also known as rapid development, is designing and implementing user interfaces that provide users with clear and

concise prompts or messages. These prompts may be error messages, notifications, confirmations, or other messages that guide users through a software application.

Prompt engineering is an essential skill for modern software developers and designers, as it can significantly improve the user experience of a product. When well-designed, prompts can help users understand what is happening within an application, provide helpful guidance when encountering errors or obstacles, and ensure that users feel confident using the software.

One of the main benefits of prompt engineering is that it can significantly reduce user frustration and confusion. When users encounter error messages or other unclear or unhelpful prompts, they may become frustrated and give up on using the application altogether. Conversely, when prompts are designed to be clear and concise, users are more likely to trust the application and continue using it.

Another benefit of prompt engineering is that it can improve the overall efficiency of a software application. When well-designed prompts help users navigate through an application more quickly and easily, reducing the time and effort required to complete tasks, this can be especially important for software applications used in professional settings, where time is often at a premium.

In addition to improving a software application's user experience and efficiency, prompt engineering can also help ensure that users are using the software correctly and safely. For example, prompts can be used to alert users to potential security risks or to ensure that users are aware of significant changes or updates to the application.

Given the importance of prompt engineering in modern software development, young people entering the workforce today must possess prompt solid engineering skills. Whether they are working as software developers, designers, or user experience specialists, these individuals will be responsible for creating functional and user-friendly software applications. Without prompt solid engineering skills, they may struggle to develop applications that meet these criteria.

Fortunately, many resources are available for young people who want to develop their prompt engineering skills. Online courses, coding boot camps, and other training programs can give individuals the knowledge and skills to create effective prompts and messages. Additionally, working on projects with experienced software developers and designers can provide valuable hands-on experience and help young people develop their skills in a real-world setting.

Overall, prompt engineering is a crucial skill for young people entering the workforce today. By developing prompt solid engineering skills, they can help ensure that the software applications they create are efficient, user-friendly, and safe for users. As the importance of software applications continues to grow in our increasingly digital world, prompt engineering will only become more critical, making it a valuable skill for any young person to possess.

SIX

Conclusion- The Requisite!

India's youth need computer skilling

The target year for achieving the Sustainable Development Goals (SDGs), signed in 2015, is 2030. While 2030 may seem a long way off, reaching the 17 goals and 169 targets is a challenge, thanks to the impact of Covid-19, the Ukraine war and sluggish global economic growth. As part of the SDG monitoring process, the National Sample Survey Office (NSSO) conducted a multiple indicator survey across 276,409 Indian households between January 2020 and August 2021 and collected data on several critical development indicators, one being working knowledge of using computers. The survey report was released on March 7.

The NSSO survey found that a large share of young Indians is ill-prepared to shift work and education online. Only 15.6% of those in the 15 and above age group could send emails with attached files, a basic skill. This number improved to only 27.5% among the younger 15-25 age group. What's more alarming is that if education was to be conducted through compact discs or other removable drives, not all students might be able to pursue education easily. Only 43% in the 15-25 age group (35% in rural areas) could copy or move a file or folder.

The lack of such basic computer skills will be a handicap for the young when they pursue education and seek employment. While there has been an uptick in digital education, it must not be confined to just online lectures and books. The NSSO survey is a reminder that India must invest more human and financial resources to train the young about platforms and new technological tools, and teach them how to exploit these skills to learn, earn, and navigate a technology-driven world.

Source: Hindustan Times, Editorial, 10th March 2023

Prompt engineering is the process of creating or modifying prompts to guide the behaviour of an AI language model. Skilling through prompt engineering involves using prompts to train the model to perform a specific task or improve its performance on a particular input type.

To skill an AI model through prompt engineering, you can follow these steps:

Identify the task you want the model to perform or the type of input you want it to improve on.

Create or modify prompts that give the model context and guide its behaviour towards the desired output.

Use the prompts to train the model on the task or input type.

Evaluate the model's performance and iterate on the prompts to refine its behaviour.

- *Fine-tune the model on specific prompts or prompt sets to improve performance on the desired task or input type.*

- *Test the model on new data to ensure it is performing well.*

Repeat the steps until the model performs at the desired level.

Prompt engineering can improve the performance of AI models on a wide range of tasks, from language generation to image classification. By carefully designing prompts and using them to train the model, you can effectively guide its behaviour towards the desired outcome and achieve better results than traditional training methods. Skilling through prompt engineering means teaching an AI language model to perform a specific task or improving its performance on a particular input type by creating or modifying prompts. Prompts are cues or hints that guide the model's behaviour towards the desired outcome.

Using prompts to train the model, you can help it learn faster and perform better on the task or input type you want to improve. You can refine the prompts based on the model's performance and keep fine-tuning it until it achieves the desired level of performance. Overall, prompt engineering is a way to make AI models smarter and more accurate in their predictions or outputs.

Creating and implementing user interfaces that offer users prompts or straightforward messages and are to the point is referred to as prompt engineering. Another name for this process is rapid development. These prompts may appear as error messages, alerts, confirmations, or any other letters that assist users in navigating their way through software applications. The user interface for this technology has to be enhanced as it becomes more widespread so that more people may benefit from it. This is when the need for rapid engineering becomes apparent. Prompt engineering aims to manage the output of the language model (an AI tool) by giving it particular context, restrictions, rules, and so on. This is done to achieve the aim of prompt engineering.

Since it can potentially enhance a product's overall user experience vastly, prompt engineering is an essential talent for current software engineers and designers. When prompts are well-designed, they may assist users in comprehending what is occurring inside an application, give helpful information when users meet mistakes or barriers and guarantee that users feel secure using the program. Several benefits can be achieved when prompts are used.

One of the primary advantages of quick engineering is that it has the potential to significantly cut down on the annoyance and misunderstanding experienced by users. Users confronted with error warnings or instructions that are ambiguous or otherwise unhelpful run the risk of becoming annoyed and ultimately giving up on using the program entirely. On the other hand, users are more likely to trust the program and continue using it when instructions are clear and concise.

The reasons why prompt engineering is the way of the future:

The number of interactions with big language models requires fast engineering, which is becoming increasingly important as the number of interactions with these models rises. It is a talent valued and sought after since it needs a mix of technical abilities and creative thinking, making it challenging to acquire.

To get the most possible benefit from more complex large-scale language models, it will be necessary to use both efficient and effective prompts. This need will grow in importance over time.

Since prompt engineering is still a reasonably young area, a local pool of experienced individuals exists. As a result, there is a larger demand for prompt engineers, which may lead to better wages.

As the usage of massive language models becomes more widespread, there will be an increased need for quick engineers to assist businesses and people in getting the most out of these practical tools.

Because of this, there will most likely be more chances available and more significant earning potential for quick engineers.

Conclusion

The activity of meticulously creating prompts to increase big language models' efficiency is called "prompt engineering."

To provide outputs from these models that are of a high quality, accurate, and helpful nature, quick engineering is going to become more crucial as the capabilities of these models continue to increase.

As a result of prompt engineering, big language models may be made to comprehend and react to a wider variety of inputs and inquiries, which makes them more flexible and suitable for a broader range of applications. Prompt engineers are responsible for carefully constructing prompts that direct the attention and concentration of the model. This helps to guarantee that the model can offer correct and relevant responses to the questions posed to it.

Also, rapid engineering may enhance big language models' overall efficiency and performance, which is a significant benefit.

Prompt engineers may assist in decreasing the amount of data and computing resources necessary to create a response by giving the model brief and focused prompts. This makes the model more efficient and cost-effective to operate, which in turn benefits the prompt engineers.

Generally, timely engineering will become an increasingly crucial discipline as big language models continue to develop and become more extensively employed in a broad range of applications. This is because large language models are expected to grow more complex. Prompt engineers may assist in guaranteeing that these models can offer correct and relevant responses to a broad variety of queries and inputs by carefully constructing prompts that steer the attention and focus of these models. Some helpful hints for efficient, quick engineering are as follows:

Be specific: Be as detailed as possible while creating your prompts. Avoid using ambiguous or general terms since they might be taken differently. You may try something like, "Write a poem about the beauty of a sunset over the ocean," as an alternative to stating, "Write a poem about nature."

Utilize context: If you want the model to provide more accurate results, include any relevant context in your questions. If you want the model to compose a poem about a specific location, for instance, you should have some background information about that location in the prompt that you provide them.

Structure: Using unambiguous language and being to the point will provide a system for your suggestions. Because of this, the model can give logically structured and simple solutions. For instance, you might try stating something like "Create a tale that starts with a character waking up on a Monday morning and ends with them finding they have a super ability" rather than "Write a story."

Be creative: Exert some imagination and whimsy in the prompts you provide. This can potentially motivate the model to create more fascinating and unique replies. Try rephrasing the prompt as "Create a short narrative about a time traveller who travels back in time to see the dinosaurs," for instance, rather than just stating, "Write a short story," so that it sounds more interesting.

Experiment: Try out various prompt types and forms, such as open-ended inquiries, fill-in-the-blank statements, or multiple-choice choices, to see which ones provide the most pertinent and correct replies from the language model.

By adhering to these pointers, you will be able to communicate with substantial language models in an efficient manner and create replies of a high calibre.

One further advantage of using rapid engineering is that it might increase the application's overall efficiency level. Prompts have the potential to assist users in navigating an application more quickly and straightforwardly, hence cutting down on the amount of time and effort needed to do tasks when they are well-designed. This may be of utmost significance for software programs utilized in professional contexts, which often have limited time to complete tasks.

In addition to enhancing the overall quality of the user experience and increasing the application's overall productivity, quick engineering may also assist in ensuring that users use the program appropriately and securely. Prompts may be used, for instance, to warn users about possible security issues or to make specific that users are informed of significant changes or upgrades made to the program.

Considering the significance of prompt engineering in creating current software, it is necessary for young individuals who are just entering the job today to possess solid abilities in prompt engineering. Whether they are employed as software developers, designers, or user experience experts, the persons in this category will be tasked with developing software programs that are functional and pleasant to the end user. They may have difficulty developing apps that satisfy these requirements if they lack significant abilities in rapid engineering.

Young individuals interested in developing their talents in the field of short engineering are fortunate to have access to many resources. Individuals may get the knowledge and skills necessary to design prompts and messages effectively by enrolling in coding boot camps, online courses, or other training programs. In addition, having young people work on projects with seasoned software engineers and designers may offer them the necessary hands-on experience and assist them in developing their talents in a setting more representative of the world.

In general, prompt engineering is an essential ability for young people who are just starting a job. They can assist in guaranteeing that the software programs they produce are practical, user-friendly, and safe for people to use if they have good abilities in prompt engineering. Because of the growing significance of software applications in our increasingly digital society, rapid engineering will only become more crucial, making it an invaluable talent that every young person should strive to acquire.

Prompting is pretty much the only skill you need now to be a master of these new large and powerful generative models, whether it be to generate extraordinary stories, striking images, or any cool feature like a text summarizer or automatic video editor tool. This is true whether you want to create remarkable stories, vivid images, or any cool part like a text summarizer or automated video editor tool.

The outcomes produced by these models continue to improve with time, but it might be challenging to get the precise information that one is seeking from them. Although this will improve, the most effective method to capitalize on the possibilities of these enormous models is to become a better prompt engineer.

The technique of deliberately constructing prompts to elicit specific answers from individuals is called "prompt engineering." It has several potential applications, such as education, marketing, psychology, etc. The following are some instances of how students and regular people might use prompt engineering in their day-to-day lives:

As you are studying, you may make use of prompts to assist you in remembering the material you have read. For instance, if you are attempting to recall a list of things, you may make a mnemonic device by utilizing the initial letter of each item in the list. Another method for evaluating one's knowledge level is to use flashcards with questions on one side and answers on the other.

To keep yourself motivated to exercise consistently, you might use suggestions. You may remind yourself to exercise regularly by setting reminders on your phone, writing out your fitness objectives, and posting them in a prominent location.

Time management: You may make better use of the time you have available to you by making use of prompts. You may, for instance, utilize a calendar or the reminder functions on your phone to ensure that you don't miss any of your appointments or other important dates.

Eating routines: If you want to promote healthier eating routines, you may use prompts. You may, for instance, put a note on your refrigerator to remind you to consume more fruits and vegetables, or you can keep a food journal to track what you consume.

You may boost your interaction with your followers and strengthen your social media presence by using prompts on social media. You may, for instance, encourage readers to participate with your information by asking questions or creating polls on your website.

In general, prompt engineering may be an effective method for assisting persons in achieving their objectives and improving the quality of their day-to-day lives.

SEVEN

QUOTES ON PROMPT ENGINEERING

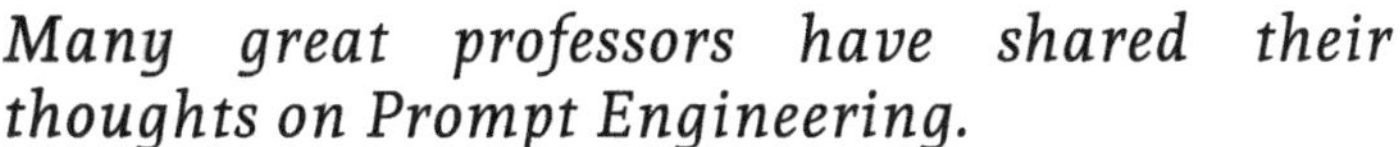

Many great professors have shared their thoughts on Prompt Engineering.

Here are a few examples:

Dr Subra Suresh, President of Nanyang Technological University and former Director of the National Science Foundation, said, "Prompt Engineering is an important and growing field critical to our society. It combines creativity, innovation, and problem-solving skills to create solutions that benefit everyone."

ᑭᑭᑭ

Dr Edward Crawley, Ford Professor of Engineering at MIT, has said, "Prompt Engineering is all about finding solutions to complex problems quickly and efficiently. It requires a deep understanding of science and technology and a willingness to collaborate with others and take risks."

ᑭᑭᑭ

Dr John Hennessy, former President of Stanford University and a computer scientist, has said, "Prompt Engineering is at the forefront of technological innovation and is critical to our economic competitiveness. It requires a strong foundation in science and engineering and an ability to think creatively and work collaboratively."

ᑭᑭᑭ

Dr Mary C. Boyce, Dean of the School of Engineering and Applied Science at Columbia University, said, "Prompt Engineering is an exciting field that offers endless opportunities to impact the world positively. It requires a passion for solving problems, working in teams, and committing to lifelong learning."

ᑭᑭᑭ

These professors, and many others like them, recognize the importance and potential of Prompt Engineering in today's world. They understand that Prompt Engineering requires technical knowledge and skills, creativity, collaboration, and a commitment to innovation.

ᑭᑭᑭ

EIGHT

About The Author

Dheeraj Mehrotra, MS, MPhil, PhD (Education Management) HC., a white and a yellow belt in SIX SIGMA, a Certified NLP Business Diploma holder, is an Educational Innovator, Author, with expertise in Six Sigma In Education, Academic Audits, Neuro-Linguistic

Programming (NLP), Total Quality Management In Education, an Experiential Educator, a CBSE Resource towards School Assessment (SQAA), CCE, JIT, Five S, and KAIZEN.

He has authored over 100 books on topics which include Computer Science, AI, Digital Body Language, NLP, Quality Circles, School Management, Classroom Effectiveness and Safety and security in schools. A former Principal at De Indian Public School, New Delhi, (INDIA), NPS International School, Guwahati, and Education Officer at GEMS, Gurgaon, with an ample teaching experience of over Two Decades, he is a certified Trainer for Quality Circles/ TQM in Education and QCI Standards for School Accreditation/ School Audits and Management. He has also been honoured with the President of India's National Teacher Award in the year 2006 and the Best Science Teacher State Award (By the Ministry of Science and Technology, State of UP), Innovation in Education for his inception of Six Sigma In Education by Education Watch, New Delhi. Presently engaged as a Principal at Kunwar's Global School, Lucknow, India.

Can be reached at www.authordheerajmehrotra.com

NINE

Books By The Same Author

iMusic · In stock
Dr Dheeraj Mehrotra · Basic...

Bookshop
Educators Success Sto...

iMusic
Artificial Intelligence (P...

Kopykitab · In stock
Step By Step Computer...

Amazon.in
Dr Dheeraj Mehrotra Dr...

Goodreads
ISC Computer Science f...

Flipkart
Setp by Step Computer ...

Kopykitab
Step Computer Learning...

Jobors.com
Dr Dheeraj Mehrotra -Who believes that ...

www.authordheerajmehrotra.com

TEN

Tips to learning Prompt Engineering

The following are some pointers that can assist you in learning "prompt engineering":

When you begin to create prompts for the language model, it is vital to first have a thorough understanding of the job that you want the language model to do. This will assist you in designing prompts that are relevant to the activity at hand and create replies of a high quality.

Begin with the basics: Start out with straightforward questions that demand the language model to carry out fundamental responsibilities, such as finishing a sentence or coming up with a condensed phrase. Both your knowledge of the fundamentals of rapid engineering and your self-assurance will increase as a result of this.

Make use of examples: Search for models of good prompts, analyze them, and figure out what it is about them that makes them successful. You will be able to enhance your own prompt engineering abilities as well as learn from the experiences of others as a result of doing this.

Test and iterate: Put your prompts through some tests to evaluate how well they do, and make adjustments to them as necessary. This will assist you in refining your prompts and increasing the efficiency of those prompts.

Be inventive: challenge conventional thinking and come up with original and imaginative ideas for prompts. Do not be scared to think outside the box. This may help you develop replies from the language model that are more intriguing and engaging for the audience.

Pay attention to customer input and incorporate it into the development of new and improved prompts by using it. This will make it easier for you to generate prompts that are more valuable and effective for the people you are trying to reach.

Maintain a current knowledge: Maintain a current knowledge of the most recent advancements in the fields of prompt engineering and natural language processing. You will be able to remain ahead of the curve and continue to enhance your talents as a result of doing this over time.

9 798890 025210

Printed by Libri Plureos GmbH in Hamburg, Germany